Top 10 Prepping Mistakes (and How to Avoid Them)

By Robert Paine

© 2014

Are You Prepared to Save Yourself and Your Family When Disaster Strikes?

Have you ever thought about prepping? And when you do, have you been a bit overwhelmed, at least once or twice? Prepping can seem like a huge task that will take too much work. But don't worry! It doesn't have to be that way.

There are common mistakes that every Prepper makes. And yet, these mistakes are so easy to correct. With this book, you'll learn the Top 10 Prepping Mistakes…and more importantly, how to avoid them!

If you are interested in learning how to protect your family from any and all of the inevitable disasters that could potentially happen, this book is your first step to learning how to prepare for any emergency situation. Get started today!

Sign up for Robert's Mailing List to be notified of **New Releases**

and **Special Sales**: http://eepurl.com/zvm11

Top 10 Prepping Mistakes (and How to Avoid Them!)

Prepping for a disaster is becoming quite trendy. Though it has always been practiced by a variety of people, over generations and generations, lately it has begun to take on a new importance. It is widely talked about and discussed freely in popular culture. There are plenty of people who are diving into prepping in an attempt to get ahead of the game, so to speak. There are also plenty of people who want to know what all the fuss is about.

Ten years ago, prepping was regarded as one of those things crazy people who lived deep in the forests did. Today, more and more people are seeing the sound reasoning behind prepping. We've seen natural disasters, governmental instability, wars and disease reaching our shores, and more. Even the government has advised every household to be prepared to live at last three days without assistance by storing food, water and other emergency gear. Clearly, there *is* something to this whole prepping thing, and more and more people are quickly catching on. With the increased interest in prepping, there are plenty of people who are a bit lost and just following the trend. They are jumping into prepping with both feet and grabbing this and that with no real purpose. It's not the most effective way!

Prepping is a little art, a little science and a lot of experience. New preppers are prone to making some big mistakes that could cost them and their families in the long run. In fact, it isn't just new preppers who are making mistakes. There are plenty of so-called veteran preppers who have gotten so focused on one thing, that they are leaving themselves vulnerable to other issues. The good news: the mistakes are fixable. However, you have to be able to identify the mistakes before you can correct them. Choosing who to listen to and follow is going to be your biggest hurdle. Ideally, you should do research and base your own decisions on the information you have gathered from various reputable sources. Don't accept anything at face value. If you are not certain about a particular statement, research it and get a second opinion. Prepping isn't all about following the latest trends and gurus, or trying to do what everybody else is doing. The best thing you can do as a prepper is to tailor and customize your prepping for YOU. Focus on you and your family and your specific needs. Everything else will fall into place.

The following pages include the top ten mistakes preppers, new and old, tend to make. They are culled from hundreds of interviews that I've done with people all over the nation over the past years. In talking with them, I see the same mistakes come up over and over again. Do yourself a favor and avoid falling into any one of these traps. Examine your current prepping habits through the lens of these common mistakes and decide which areas you need to change. You may just be saving your life and the lives of your family members by avoiding these practices. You *will* definitely save yourself a lot of frustration when the event you have been preparing for actually happens. Too often, we discover mistakes too late. And in the prepping game, that can mean the difference between surviving or not. But this is not new, completely unknown advice. There are others out there who have found out these mistakes so that you don't have to. You don't need to reinvent the prepping wheel. Learn from other's mistakes!

#1 - Focusing On Just One Type of Prepper Event

This is a big one. One of the most common mistakes known in the prepping world. If you have ever checked out some blogs or watched *that* famous prepping show on television, you have probably noticed the person writing the blog or featured on the program was focused on one particular situation that could thrust the country into a world where it would truly be survival of the fittest and most prepared. One situation only. Their entire prep is geared towards only one possible event happening. See the mistake yet?

Focusing all of your energy on preparing for a pandemic will leave you vulnerable to an event like a total collapse of the dollar or the power grid. What if you're prepping for governmental collapse and then, whoops, along comes a huge natural disaster? While some preps are interchangeable, you will notice some people will spend a lot of their time, energy, and money investing in biohazard suits, plastic sheets and face masks to ride out a pandemic, but ignore things like backup power sources or avoid stocking up on items that can be used for bartering. What good is a biohazard suit going to do you if the collapse stems from the power grid going down?

There are plenty of events that could turn our world upside down. Natural disasters. Governmental collapse. Power grids going down. Wars. Medical emergencies. And on and on. So, it should go without saying, we have no way of predicting what will be the cause of the next big event where prepping will come into play. Keep your preps rather generic and you will be better off. Ensuring you are prepared for anything is the best way to go. Don't get too hung up on one specific potential event. Getting too specific in your prepping will leave you vulnerable to *all* of the other possible hazards that could come our way. These are some of the things that could leave you on your own and fighting to survive.

- Foreign or domestic war
- EMP (electro-magnetic pulse)
- Government collapse
- Power Grid failure
- Natural Disaster
- Diseases
- Dollar collapse

There is always the risk you will be faced with a combination of events. For example, as we've seen in the past few years, when there is a major natural disaster, it usually causes the power grid to fail. People who were not prepared will take to the streets to find or fight for what they need, creating a need for martial law. It's not speculation. We've seen it happen, over and over throughout the past 10 years. It only takes one disaster to set off a chain of events. You have to be ready to deal with anything and everything.

Obviously you cannot prep for every single possible event in the entire world. That's not what I'm suggesting. But you *can* and *should* prep items or prep in a way that will allow you to use your prep and your skills in a variety of events. Don't become too focused on one single, solitary event happening. You'll better your chances of survival if you prep for multiple events. Remember: look at the big picture!

#2 - Relying Only on Yourself (and Ignoring Like-Minded Others)

Another major misconception is that your prepping should be top-secret information, not to be shared with anybody except for your immediate family members. This is actually dangerous. Can you do everything *all* by yourself? Do you really want to be a lone survivor? Or, do you want to try and fight off a gang of bandits by yourself? What happens if you get injured? Who will take over until you're back to full-strength. Or, God forbid, what happens if you're no longer around? Who will take care of your family? Or will they know how to survive because you've taught them well? Keeping your prepping a secret helps nobody and potentially does a great deal of harm to you and your loved ones. So, why do you keep it secret?

A lot of people don't talk about the fact they are a prepper simply because they are worried they will be stereotyped. This may happen - there is no doubt about that. But it isn't something you should let bother you! Preppers are often made fun of and people think they are stockpiling weapons and preparing for the sky to fall. While in some ways they are right, the people who are prepping are doing so to save themselves and their families from very real and possible scenarios. And who do you think people will turn to in times of crisis? The preppers, of course!

You would be surprised to learn how many preppers there truly are out there. Sometimes, people just need to be turned onto the world of prepping. When they realize that their neighbors next door, who go to work, take their kids to soccer and have backyard barbecues and are by all accounts "normal", it helps chip away at that stereotype. People can be perfectly normal citizens and still prepare their family to get through any disaster.

Many people *are* preppers and don't even realize it. We all have that friend or family member who keeps a few months worth of food supplies in a pantry. Ask them why they have so much food and they'll say things like "Oh, it was on sale" or "Oh, this way I don't have to go out shopping in the winter weather". They wouldn't call themselves a prepper, but they sure are acting like one!

There are many simple ways to let others know about your prepping habits, and to even get them involved. Start bringing up the idea of prepping in casual conversation with your neighbors or friends. Get a read on what they think. If they are open to discussing it, talk with them about how you can work together to prepare your homes and families. Picture your neighborhood or town after a catastrophic event. You are probably not a doctor, gardener, handyman and electrician. But, your neighbors and friends probably have different skills than you do. Combining your skills and relying on each other is one sure way you can ensure you will survive and prosper following a devastating event. Dividing up responsibilities like, hunting, manning a fire or keeping watch allows you to get the rest you need in order to stay healthy.

Community is human nature. We want to be able to talk to others about what we are dealing with and we want to bounce ideas off people who can give us a different perspective. By forming your community early on, you are setting yourself up for success. You are taking a divide and conquer approach to survival. If your children have other children to play with or talk with, you will all be a lot happier.

If you know your home isn't a good place to hunker down in, but your neighbor has a basement that would make an excellent retreat, you need to ask about bringing your family into the neighbor's basement. Talk about what you can bring to the table in skills, supplies and moral support. In many situations, it makes more sense to keep a few families together in order to conserve heat and resources.

Generally, people are going to be much more open to the idea of prepping if someone they know, respect, or care about brings it up. This is our duty as preppers. We can't let our friends and loved ones think that all preppers are a bunch of nutcases. We need to let them know that what they see on TV or read on the Internet isn't true about every prepper. That, deep down, prepping is about protecting yourself and your loved ones, and that it is most successful if you can get others involved. When people see it this way, they're a lot more open-minded and usually even ready to join in and help in whatever ways they can. If you keep your prepping a secret, you'll miss out on these opportunities to strengthen yourself, your family, and your future.

#3 - Preparing Mostly to Bug Out (Instead of Bugging In)

In the prepping world, you read and see a lot about bugging out or getting out of dodge when it hits the fan. Everyone is focused on packing the absolute best bug out bag, having multiple escape plans, safe houses, and meet up locations. Don't get me wrong: those are all good things to be thinking about and even preparing for. But focusing on that is missing the entire other half of the equation.

What if you can't leave your house? What if there is a severe storm or there is an army forcing you to hunker down in your home? Are you prepared to survive in your current location? One of the biggest misconceptions people have about preppers and prepping in general is that a bug out bag is the main component of prepping. There is this idea that as soon as you hear the first siren or hear of civil unrest, you grab your bag and start running. This is a dangerous belief!

A bug out bag is definitely worth devoting some effort to, but you need a contingency plan. The bug out bag *cannot* be your only plan. What if you really cannot leave your house? Honestly, if you didn't have to, would you really want to in the first place? Your home has all the creature comforts you could want. You can stockpile food, water, blankets and other emergency gear in your home without worrying if it will fit into your backpack. Wouldn't you feel a lot safer in the familiar confines of home, rather than out in the elements, on the run, not sure where you will end up every night. Depending on the situation that has caused a prepping event, many times staying at home is the much, much better choice.

The goal of preparing for anything is just that – a goal. You can't assume you will automatically leave your home and head out into the great blue yonder, no matter what. You need to prepare to bug in as well. Spend some time developing plans for either scenario. Ideally, if you can stay in your home, that should be your first option. This will take care of your need to find shelter and give you some time to evaluate the situation. It will also eliminate the line of foot and vehicle traffic that is likely exiting the city. Don't get too caught up in the excitement of bugging out. Sure it's fun to build a bug out bag and imagine yourself out in the wild, in the elements, building a fire and hunting your food. But think about it – is that *really* the most ideal situation? Definitely not. Take the time to evaluate the situation and choose the plan that is best for your family.

Focusing solely on bugging out can also leave you vulnerable, especially in extreme weather conditions. One of your first priorities when bugging out is finding shelter. It doesn't make a lot of sense to head out into a snowstorm or hurricane simply because you have been practicing and focusing on bugging out and your bug out bag is all ready. You will find that most plans involve both, hunkering down and bugging out. Depending on the situation, where you live, and what your secondary location looks like, you will likely need to hunker down and wait until it is safe to move or move and then hunker down. So don't focus all of your time, efforts, and money on bugging out now. Plan for both, prepare for both, stock items for both, and practice both. That way you'll be ready to survive, no matter what the situation.

#4 - Having a Lot of Gear (But Not Knowing How to Use It)

Did you spend some time surfing the net or trolling your local army surplus stores finding some really cool gear? You've narrowed down your choices, read all of the reviews, and thought that you absolutely needed this thing for your prepping? You probably read the packaging and decided each piece was definitely a necessity to your survival and you paid for it not truly understanding what it was. Maybe you reasoned that the packaging included the face of a dude who is famous for his survival skills so if his face is on it, it must be really good, right? Or you assume the pictures on the packaging are pretty self-explanatory and how hard could it really be to use it when the time comes?

This is a common and costly prepping mistake. Unfortunately, many preppers buy everything but the kitchen sink and shove it into their bug out bag or stock it in their basement with the rest of their emergency supplies. They then forget about it completely and it sits there gathering dust. Some of the gear can be very expensive. Some people assume that the price obviously reflects how valuable it is and it must be worth every penny if a famous dude wearing camo uses it. Big mistake! That isn't exactly true. In fact, there are plenty of marketing experts who are aware of the prepping movement and who are taking advantage of people's lack of knowledge and creating various doodads marketed for survival and making a boatload of cash. Sadly, many of the pieces of gear are completely unnecessary or make claims that are not entirely true. There are some tools that are nothing more than a glorified screwdriver but sell for the price of a small car.

Don't rush out and buy a bunch of gear and shove it in the basement or your bug out bag and forget about it. The most fancy, shiniest, and most expensive tools do not use themselves. Price does not necessarily reflect quality or usefulness. And, remember, you still have to know how to use all of that gear you are buying. Don't assume you will figure it out when the time comes. You don't have time to be learning anything new in a survival situation.

First off, stop buying single-use gear, whenever possible. Buy gear that serves many purposes and can be reused for multiple tasks. Do spend extra money buying a quality piece of gear rather than a cheap counterpart that will break after a couple of uses. Practice with it often in a variety of conditions. Try using it in the dark, when it is raining outside or when the wind is blowing. Professional basketball players don't show up on the court and assume a basketball is pretty self-explanatory and they don't need to actually mess with the ball until game day. You have to practice and get familiar with the quirks of your gear and how it works the best for you. Practice makes perfect is my prepping mantra and it should be yours too. Don't be the only member of your family who knows how to use the tools either. Give everyone a chance to practice and become familiar with the tools. You're all going to need to know how to use survival tools when the time comes, so the time to start practicing is now.

When you are practicing with your gear, you are going to become so familiar with using it that it will become second nature. This is what we want. You will know how far you can push it before it breaks. You will know it's little quirks and tips and tricks. It will also give you the opportunity to think of other uses for the tool. If you can eliminate a second tool from your bug out bag, you are making a little more room for an extra granola bar or bottle of water.

Do not make the mistake of more is better. More can get you killed. Having so much gear that you can't move freely because you are weighed down by a stuffed bug out bag or you can't find the tool you need in a hurry is a recipe for disaster. The motto for your prepping tools should be: simple and useful. Don't buy the newest gear just because you saw it on TV or read about it somewhere. Don't fall into the consumerism trap of thinking you *need* the newest gadget, when something you already have will do the same exact job. Know what tools you have. Know how to use the tools you have. Make sure your family or friends know how to use the tools. Stay away from buying flashy things just because they're new and shiny.

#5 - Storing All of Your Preps in the Same Place

You have heard the phrase, "Don't put all of your eggs into one basket." Well, in the world of prepping, we can translate that to say, "Don't put all your preps in one place." Don't load your basement with every bit of your supplies. What happens if your house is destroyed or your basement floods? All of your time, money and hard work will be for naught. Your food and lifeline will be gone. Don't put all of your gear in the garage – what if a fire strikes? Don't put everything in your bug out bag – what if that gets lost? You get the idea. Everything in one place is nothing but a recipe for disaster. And it's something that can be so easily avoided.

You want to spread the wealth, so to speak. Spread the gear. Spread the prep! You should have second options for just about everything, wherever possible. As part of your prepping plan, you should have a secondary location chosen for your family to bug out to in case your home is compromised. You will need to keep supplies in both locations. If you don't have a second home or cabin to retreat to, consider burying supplies in an area where you plan to bug out to or even around your backyard. Make sure you mark the area in a way you will notice, but others will not.

Keep gear in each one of your vehicles, in your desk drawer at work and along the route you would take to get from work to home in an emergency. This may sound like overkill, but you have to consider ALL the disasters that could occur and leave you and your family in a survival situation. You don't have to store a year's worth of food and water in every location. Simply put in a few bottles of water, a knife and a way to start fire. That is all you really need to get started on your survival journey.

If you are working with friends or neighbors, you may want to consider distributing supplies to their homes as well. This is risky, but if you trust the people, do it. You are probably safe putting things at your sister's, brother's or parent's house to use. If your family members are not on board with your prepping, think twice before putting your supplies in their home. You don't want them to borrow your food when they are making dinner or entertaining guests.

You also want to be careful storing your preps in one place in case your home is broken into by people intent on taking what you have. If you have everything in one place like your pantry or basement, looters are going to take it all. By placing preps throughout your home in not-so-obvious places, you are ensuring you will have something left if you are robbed. Looters are not going to waste a lot of time searching your home top to bottom. If they find a stash of food in the pantry, they are going to assume that is it and move on. Little do they know you have a couple boxes in the garage labeled "Christmas decorations" that are actually filled with water and food.

Too often, people will spend a whole lot of time, money, and effort building up a great prep. They'll load it up with food, water, and all other kinds of necessary supplies. They go through all of that trouble, only to store it all in one, single location. Big mistake! Don't do that to yourself. Don't waste your prepping efforts by not having a backup location. You've done everything else right up to this point, so do the simple, smart thing, and spread your prep around. It doesn't have to be spread into ten different places or intricately buried around town with a treasure map. Keep it simple, but keep it separated. You'll thank yourself later.

#6 - Not Rotating Your Food Supplies

If you have been adding food to your emergency food storage for several months already, you may be guilty of this. It's something simple but something that a lot of people can easily overlook. You have to rotate your food! If the world around you does come crashing in and you are forced to rely on that food you have been storing, what will you do when you discover it is spoiled? Spoiled to the point it would be potentially deadly to eat? All that work for naught. Look – grocery stores rotate food. Restaurants rotate food. So why wouldn't you?

There is a rule you must follow when you are building up your food storage—FIFO. FIFO stands for first in, first out. When you are adding new cans or other food to your shelves, pull the old stuff forward and put the new stuff in back. Take the time to check the condition of the cans, boxes and bags of food you have on your shelf. Check the expiration dates. If something is out of date, pull it out of your food storage and replace it with a fresh item. If something is coming really close to being out of date, pull it and use it for dinner. You can replace it with a fresh one and still get use out of the old one before it spoils. Best of both worlds.

Technically, a best by date means just that. It's a date that, ideally, the food is most fresh, or best used by. The box of crackers with a best by date is a guideline. If you open it up after the best by date, you are probably going to discover the crackers are stale. They are safe to eat, but they are just not as great a quality as they would have been before that date. The dates on your food are put there by the manufacturers as a quality control mechanism and as a way to cover their own behinds. They don't want to sell food that is past its prime. It is, however, just a guideline, and not a hard and fast rule.

Although you can technically eat most food that has gone past its expiration date, you do need to be careful. Look for signs the food is spoiled. Cans of food that are leaking, bulging or have a nasty odor when you open them up should never be consumed. Do your best to keep your food stores fresh by pulling out food that is close to its expiration and using it in your daily meals. Replace what you took and you will ensure you are keeping a fresh supply of food. You never know when disaster will strike so you want to stay on top of the rotation. Commit to checking your food storage at least once a month. If it helps, keep a running inventory on a spreadsheet. Print off the spreadsheet and keep it in your purse or wallet. The next time you go to the grocery store, you will know what supplies are running low or are close to expiring. This can help you avoid having 20 cans of corn and a single can of green beans on hand.

Take care in choosing storage spaces that are conducive to long shelf lives. Avoid extreme heat or cold, moisture and direct sunlight. Do your best to manage pests to keep them from getting in and spoiling your food. Invest in 5-gallon food grade buckets and Mylar bags. You can extend the shelf life of things like dried grains and beans and pastas for years when you seal the food in Mylar bags.

Use common sense when rotating and stocking your pantry. Obviously some things are going to have a much shorter shelf life than others. If you have any baked products, dairy, refrigerated meats or produce, those are going to go bad much more quickly than canned goods, dried goods, jerky, or things of that nature. Rotate their stocks more often and use the older goods more frequently.

This is a task that you can really get your whole family involved in. Some kids don't like certain prepping tasks, but some really love dealing with food and the pantry. Make it into a fun game. Get a clipboard and some paper and teach them how to make a log of the pantry items, with bought dates, best-by dates, used dates, and things such as that. Have one of their chores be checking the pantry, keeping an eye on dates and suggesting which items you should use, which items you need to buy more of, and which items need to be rotated. This will really help them feel involved in the family prepping process and is a great way to teach them skills that will help in all areas of their lives. Which leads us to the next common mistake that preppers make…

#7 - Not Getting the Entire Family Involved

You don't have to prep alone. In fact, you *shouldn't* be prepping alone. Not if you have a family. Do not try to be the hero in your family. Every person in your family should be involved in your prepping. You don't have to send the kids to the grocery store to buy a bunch of canned food for your food storage, but you do need to have them help you do the rotation and stock the shelves. They need to know where the food is and what they should eat just in case you are not there when things go sideways.

It is a good idea to delegate various tasks to help take some of the workload off you while getting the family involved. You need every hand to help out when things go bad. Your kids, wife, husband or whatever will all play a vital role in the ultimate survival of the whole family. Talk with your children about what they need to do if they hear the sirens go off or if you call them and tell them it's time. You don't want to spend precious minutes explaining what needs to happen in the real event. Run drills to help them remember what it is they are supposed to do when you sound the alarm. This allows you to focus on doing other things because you know the rest of the family is doing what they are supposed to. Working together as a team ups your odds for survival tremendously.

If you have nearby relatives, get them involved too. It will be an all hands on deck situation when the real situation unfolds. Work together to create plans for bugging out, bugging in and what escape routes you will use. Each family member needs to know what to do. You cannot be with them every second of the day. Not telling them what to do, where to go or what gear to use is setting them up for failure. They may grumble a bit and chalk your desire for them to be involved as crazy, but that crazy just may save their lives. Explain to them why you are prepping, why you are practicing, and why they need to be involved. You don't need to scare them, but they do need to understand the importance of it and how they fit into the overall survival plan.

You also have to plan for the worst. If you are incapacitated, you are going to be relying on your family to pick up the slack. What if you have to leave out of town and the world falls apart while you are hundreds of miles away from your family? They have to know what to do and where to find the supplies you have been building up.

You also need to think of the future. Depending on the severity of the crisis, you could be living on your wits and skill for a year or more. Your family will feel better if they are prepared to live without running water or electricity. If they are thrust into the situation without a clue as to how they will survive, it will wreak havoc on their mental health. Survival is just as much mental as it is physical. If they panic or give up, they will surely fall victim to the catastrophe.

You can help eliminate the fear of living in a different world by training and preparing them for doing things a little differently. They will not be as scared and will be more capable of helping out. It will give them a purpose and a feeling of accomplishment. You don't want them sitting around fretting over their circumstances.

Give them the tools they need to thrive. Remember: the family that preps together, survives together!

#8 - Not Having the Skills to Live Sustainability

Another huge mistake preppers make is by loading up on food and water and kicking back, waiting for the sky to fall. Without doing anything else. So, what if the catastrophic event that happens is so severe that the world will take several years to right itself? Do those preppers have enough food and water on hand to last three years? Not likely. Do they have the skills to survive once their current stash runs out? Even less likely. Most preppers think they have enough food and water to last them a year when, in fact, they only have enough to last about six months. So, they survived the first six months following a disaster, now what?

You cannot assume you have stored enough to get you by indefinitely. An emergency food storage is only half the battle. It's meant for emergencies, not long-term survival of years or more. You have to be prepared for the almost unthinkable event that may wipe out your food storage before you ever get the chance to use it or for an event that lasts a whole lot longer than you had originally prepped for.

You need to learn some valuable skills that will keep you alive when the food runs out. Take the time to learn and practice how to hunt, fish and forage. The vast majority of the population has no idea how to do any of these things. If you learn even one of them, you'll be at a much greater advantage when the time comes for you to use those skills. You also need to try your hand at gardening, if you have never done so in the past. It can seem intimidating at first, but if you learn the basics, you'll find that it's not too difficult to grow enough food to supplement your pantry at least. Depending on your climate, you can grow an amazingly large variety of fruits, vegetables, tubers, and more. Think about cities you have lived in or where you live now – how many people actually have a garden? How far ahead of the pack would you be if you had a garden and knew how to use it?

If you don't have a big yard or live in an apartment, you can still grow things in containers. Read up about patio gardening and you'll find a whole wealth of information to get you started. Just on a balcony or deck alone, you can grow all kinds of lettuce, tomatoes, peas, and more. Don't forget to add heirloom seeds to your preps. You have to start somewhere. Along with typical summer gardening, you will want to learn how to grow food in the winter months as well, if your climate demands it. Look into what it takes to make a greenhouse out of scraps laying around the house. Odds are that you will already have a lot of the necessary material or could easily obtain it. Cold frames are another option you will want to read about. This ensures you have a source of food all year round. You should take up gardening and hunting even if you have food on hand to supplement your supplies. Don't wait to figure it out when the food runs out.

Hunting doesn't necessarily require you to use a gun. If you are relying on a gun to hunt game, you need to have extra ammunition on hand. Plus, you better practice your shot – it's not as easy as it looks. Shooting a running animal is difficult. Many experts will advise you leave the big game alone and focus your efforts on small animals that tend to be more abundant and a lot easier to procure. You will want to learn how to build traps and snares and how to fish without the luxury of a fancy rod and reel. You cannot survive on meat alone and will need to learn what plants are safe to eat. There are hundreds of edibles that are often viewed as weeds in today's world. Those weeds may just keep you alive someday. It would be a good idea to include a book of edible plants in your emergency preps. There are a lot of lookalike plants out there. Some are toxic. Better safe than sorry. The time to start studying is now! Get the whole family involved and you can make it fun. Spot the edible plant. Build a trap together. Learn to love fishing as a group. These are all skills that will help you survive and thrive in any catastrophic event.

Last, but certainly not least, you also need to know how to find water and then clean the water to make it safe to drink. You can (and should) add purifying tablets to your pantry. They're relatively cheap, extremely useful, and may just save your life. Eventually, though, even those will run out, if the survival event stretches on longer than you had imagined. Try to plan a safe house near freshwater, if at all possible. If you own land, build up a well or two. These are the types of investments that will pay off far into the future.

Read up on how to create catchment systems that allow you to catch rainwater instead of journeying out into the forest or urban areas to find water. Everyone will have the same plan and needs and it may get dangerous if you have to go out searching for water. If you can avoid this situation, you should plan now to be able to do so. Water is an absolute necessity and should be your biggest concern. You don't want to wake up one day and realize you have just drunk your last bottle of water and you don't have a clue as to where to find more. Plan early, plan often, plan now!

#9 - Always Believing the 'Experts' (Hint...Don't Do It!)

This is a tough one for many people. They watch TV or read books or blog and think that everyone they come across knows what they are talking about. But not every survival expert is really a survival expert (shocking, I know!). Always read carefully and realize who the source of the information is. Is it someone looking to sell you something? Someone who wants you to watch a certain TV show?

The simple fact is that a lot of these so-called experts make prepping a lot more complicated, and expensive, then it really needs to be. You don't have to have a bunch of gear to survive. You don't have to have 5-years worth of expensive freeze-dried food sitting on your shelf to ensure survival. You don't need the latest 99-in-1 tool which, oh, by the way, costs only $199!

There are always going to people trying to sell you stuff you don't need. It may not all be snake oil, but you certainly don't need a gold-plated multi-functional tool with your engraved initials. Keep it simple and you will be better off. Getting a bunch of complicated fancy gear is more dangerous than only having a single knife. The fancier the gear is, the bigger the learning curve and the more things that can go wrong with it. You will also develop a false sense of security if you surround yourself with all of the latest gadgets. You may assume that all is good because you have that cool tool that the expert said you needed. When that tool is lost or it fails, you are in big trouble. You will not have studied or practiced what to do without that tool, and you'll be paying for it, big time.

It isn't like there is a universal test that survivalists take to become an expert. Anybody can claim to be an expert without ever having stepped food in the forest or without actually starting a fire from nothing more than a couple of sticks. The term expert is used rather loosely. Use your common sense when you are reading or listening to somebody explain how to survive a disaster. Are they speaking from experience? Are they saying believable things? Are they trying to sell you something at the end of the day (and if so, run!).

Don't get caught up in a lot of hype. Most of the gadgets that are marketed towards preppers can be made with your own two hands for a fraction of the price. Or you can find a much cheaper, just as effective replacement. You don't have to spend a lot of money on gadgets and gizmos. You don't have to have specific brands of gear or a bunch of fancy kitchen tools to cook your meals. When you see a particular piece of gear that looks promising, take some time to research it. Read comments and reviews from others who have actually tried it. You don't want all the marketing hype. You want real information from real people who have used the tool or have come up with cheaper alternatives that are just as effective.

Buying food and gear should be your priority. If you can spend $20 on a bunch of food or $20 on a single tool that you may use once or twice, you have to consider which one will get you the most bang for your buck. Above all, remember: the tools and gadgets you buy are only as good as the user behind them…which will be you! Spend the time to learn your tools and you will be so much more effective with them than if you had just bought the newest, most expensive, flashiest gear!

#10 – Forgetting to Have Backups for Your Backups

What's the prepper's mantra? Always Be Prepared. I'll add to that: Always Be Prepared…and then prepare some more! We have no way of what's going to happen in the future. All we can do is plan to the best of our abilities. And that means having multiple plans. You can never have too much food or water. You can never have too many escape routes. Too many emergency contacts. Too many safe houses. You can never prepare too much. One of the main reasons we prep is because we want to prepare for almost any and everything. You cannot possibly predict what will happen in the future, of course. Therefore, you must have a plan A, B, C and so on. For every plan you come up with, you must have an option just in case something goes wrong. If you are planning on escaping the city via the highway and the highway becomes blocked, you need an alternative route. If the back road you planned on using is filled with aggressive people, you need another route and so on.

If your food storage is somehow destroyed, stolen or you can't get to it, you need to have backups in another location. There are so many different possible scenarios, it is almost impossible to predict every eventuality. You have to do your best to back up each one of your back ups. If you are not prepared with a contingency plan, you have to be ready to improvise.

Consider your bug out bag. Maybe you packed a box of waterproof matches as a way to get a fire going. Somewhere along the way, the matches fell out of your pack. Your back up plan would be your flint rod. If that is gone, then you must be prepared to make a bow drill. Prepare, prepare, prepare! Never assume everything will go according to plan or like you practiced. In reality, nothing ever goes exactly as you had trained for. Being prepared and being able to improvise is your best bet at making it through a disaster.

If you have decided to stock up on waterproof matches as your method of starting a fire, back it up with flint rod and steel. Back that up with a lighter. Back up your lighter with some steel wool and a battery. Lastly, learn how to make a bow drill. Fire is life. You can't afford not to have a backup plan when the first few options fail.

A great way to brainstorm for potential ideas that you may have missed is to get your entire family involved. Make it a fun game. Ask a question, such as: How do we get to Grandma's house if the freeway is closed? Let your children or spouse ponder it and see what they come up with. Oftentimes, they will come up with a solution that you may not have even considered. So not only is it a useful exercise, but it can be quite fun as well. It helps get everyone thinking one or two steps ahead, and that is exactly the mentality that will help you all survive when it comes down to it.

Conclusion

Prepping doesn't have to be complicated. You don't need to follow a bunch of rules or advice from so-called 'experts' on TV. What you *do* need to do is tailor your prepping for *you* and your specific experience. Hopefully now that you are aware of these 10 Prepping Mistakes that most people make, at some point, you can avoid them completely. If you can steer clear of these common pitfalls, you will already be far ahead of the pack with your prepping habits. Not only that, but you'll save time, money, and energy – all things that will be better spent on prepping activities that are actually helpful to you!

Your prepping will constantly be evolving with changes in your family, changes in your neighborhood and most importantly, changes in the current events of the world, of the country, of the state, and of your surroundings. Go with the flow and do your best to avoid making one of these costly mistakes. Constantly evaluate your preps and work to make them better. You can always improve on things. Hone your skills and be prepared. It the day never comes that you have to use your preps, count yourself fortunate, but make sure that you and your family are prepared to deal with any event that may happen in your lifetime. Pass on and share your wisdom, and keep the prepping tradition alive and well. You and your family will be much better off for it.

Stay calm. Stay in control. Stay ahead of the game. Follow these tips and avoid the mistakes above, and you will be well on your way.

Good luck, fellow Preppers!

*****

If you've enjoyed this book, **please** consider leaving a review and letting others know what you thought!

Sign up for Robert's Mailing List to be notified of **New Releases** and **Special Sales**: http://eepurl.com/zvm11

No Spam – he promises!

Other Books by Robert Paine:
Prepper's Pantry: A Survival Food Guide
The Survivalist Cookbook - Recipes for Preppers
Prepping 101: A Beginner's Survival Guide
The Dead Road: The Complete Collection

www.ingramcontent.com/pod-product-compliance
Lightning Source LLC
Chambersburg PA
CBHW070513290526
45790CB00003B/1226